MOUNTAINS

Melanie Waldron

Chicago, Illinois

www.capstonepub.com
Visit our website to find out more information about Heinemann-Raintree books.

To order:
☎ Phone 800-747-4992

💻 Visit www.capstonepub.com to browse our catalog and order online.

Edited by Nancy Dickmann, Kristen Kowalkowski, and Claire Throp
Designed by Philippa Jenkins
Original illustrations © Capstone Global Library Ltd 2013
Illustrations by Oxford Designers and Illustrators, and Words and Publications
Picture research by Tracy Cummins
Originated by Capstone Global Library Ltd
Printed and bound in China by CTPS

16 15 14 13 12
10 9 8 7 6 5 4 3 2 1

Library of Congress Cataloging-in-Publication Data
Waldron, Melanie.
  Mountains / Melanie Waldron.
    p. cm.—(Habitat survival)
  Includes bibliographical references and index.
  ISBN 978-1-4109-4597-6 (hb)—ISBN 978-1-4109-4606-5 (pb) 1. Mountains—Juvenile literature. I. Title.
  GB512.W34 2013
  577.5'3—dc23   2012000235

Acknowledgments
We would like to thank the following for permission to reproduce photographs: FLPA pp. 5 (Peter Schickert), 6, 25 (ImageBroker/Imagebroker), 11 (Sumio Harada/Minden Pictures), 15 (Konrad Woteh), 24 (Cyril Ruoso), 26 (David Hosking); iStockphoto pp. 17 (© Dennis Donohue), 18 (© martb), 20 (© michael1959); Nature Picture Library pp. 7 (Eric Baccega), 12 (Paul Hobson), 13 (Barrie Britton); Shutterstock pp. 8 (© Christopher Jackson), 9 (© Steffen Foerster Photography), 10 (© David Thyberg), 19 (© gnomeandi), 21 (© filographix), 22 (© Lee Prince), 27 (© Dennis Donohue), 29 (© Jim Lopes).

Cover photograph of an alpine ibex in Gran Paradiso National Park, Italy, reproduced with permission of Nature Picture Library/Wild Wonders of Europe/E. Haarberg.

Every effort has been made to contact copyright holders of any material reproduced in this book. Any omissions will be rectified in subsequent printings if notice is given to the publisher.

Contents

Some words are shown in bold, **like this**. You can find out what they mean by looking in the glossary.

Living in the Mountains

Around one-fifth of the land on Earth (not including the polar regions) is covered by mountains. Most of these mountains were created when large parts of Earth's surface collided together and the surface was pushed upward.

There are large mountain **ranges** on most **continents**. The Rocky Mountains run down the western side of North America, and the Alps stretch across many countries in Europe. The largest mountain range is the Himalayas, in Asia.

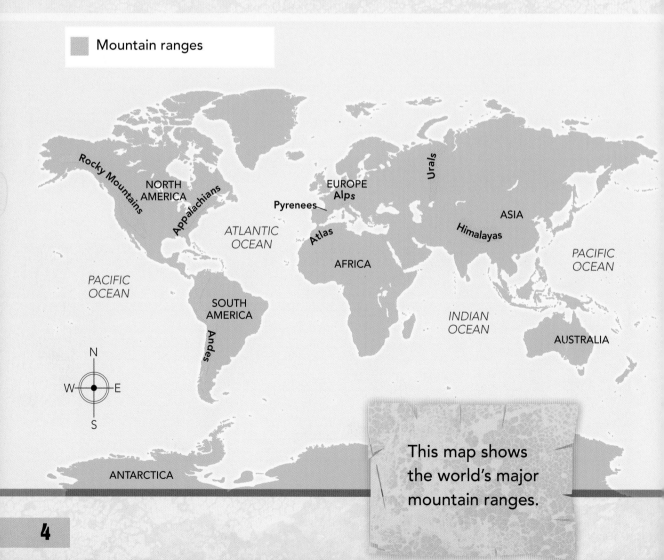

■ Mountain ranges

Rocky Mountains

NORTH AMERICA

Appalachians

Pyrenees

EUROPE
Alps

Urals

ATLANTIC OCEAN

Atlas

ASIA

Himalayas

PACIFIC OCEAN

AFRICA

PACIFIC OCEAN

SOUTH AMERICA

Andes

INDIAN OCEAN

AUSTRALIA

N
W   E
S

ANTARCTICA

This map shows the world's major mountain ranges.

Mountain plants and animals live just below the high peaks.

Mountain survival

Plants and animals living in mountains have to cope with cold weather and strong winds. The land can be very steep, and the soil can be very thin. In many places there is no soil at all, just bare rock. In very high mountains, the air is thin. This means that it has less **oxygen**. So how do plants and animals survive?

The big seven!

These are the highest mountains on each continent:

Continent	Mountain	Height
Asia	Everest	29,035 feet (8,848 meters)
South America	Aconcagua	22,841 feet (6,962 meters)
North America	Denali	20,321 feet (6,194 meters)
Africa	Kilimanjaro	19,340 feet (5,895 meters)
Europe	Elbrus	18,510 feet (5,642 meters)
Oceania	Irian Jaya	16,500 feet (5,030 meters)
Antarctica	Vinson	16,066 feet (4,897 meters)

How Do Plants Survive?

Plants growing in mountain **habitats** need to be able to cope with low temperatures. Even mountains close to the **equator**, such as Mount Kenya, get very cold at the top. This is because the air is so thin that the heat from the Sun simply escapes. Some plants contain chemicals to stop them from freezing. Others, such as the giant lobelia, have hairy stems and leaves to keep them warm.

Dead leaves

The giant groundsel grows in the mountains of East Africa. Its stem is covered with old, dead leaves, which do not fall to the ground. Instead they help to protect the plant from freezing temperatures at night.

Hug the ground

Diapensia is a plant that has **adapted** well to mountain life. It grows very low on the ground, and its leaves bind together to form a tight mat. This helps to protect it from the wind.

Wind

The strong winds in mountainous areas pose a different problem for plants. Wind not only threatens to rip plants from the ground, it also dries up their leaves. Many plants combat the wind by growing in cracks in the rock, or growing very low on the ground. Waxy leaves help to stop the drying effect of the wind.

Many Different Habitats

If you stood at the bottom of a mountain and looked up, you would see lots of different zones. At the bottom of mountain slopes, there are often forests. Here the slopes are less steep and the weather is less harsh. Further up, there are fewer trees and more meadow areas. Even higher up, there are large rocky patches. Near the top there is bare rock, and often this is covered by snow all year round. These different zones contain different **habitats**.

High up a mountain, trees can no longer grow. The place they stop growing is called the tree line.

In rocky mountainous areas, plants can **adapt** to grow in some amazing places.

Growing together

Scientists have discovered that plants growing in mountainous areas can help each other by growing close together. Some plants are good at providing shade and shelter. Some are good at trapping water and **nutrients**. Others have spiky leaves to prevent animals from eating them. If different plants grow close together, they can all help each other survive.

How Do Animals Survive?

Imagine living with freezing temperatures and ferocious winds. Imagine having to climb along steep, rocky slopes to find food. This is what life is like for many mountain animals. How have they **adapted** to these challenges?

Many animals grow thick fur to keep them warm, such as the hyrax on Mount Kenya. These are little rabbit-sized creatures, which live in gaps in the rocks.

Guanacos live high in the Andes Mountains in South America. They have very soft, thick hair to keep them warm.

Hairy feet

The Himalayan panda has hair on the soles of its feet. This protects the feet from the cold, and it also stops the panda from slipping on snow and ice.

Rock lovers

Some animals are very skilled at moving around on steep, rocky slopes. Snakes and lizards live in and around rocky areas. They warm themselves on sunbaked rocks.

The mountain goat has strong, small hooves. These help it to move around on very steep, rocky slopes.

Living the High Life

In the summertime, many mountain meadows come alive with butterflies and other insects flying among the flowers. However, they take care not to fly too high. This is to avoid the strong winds. Many mountain minibeasts live and move around the low-growing plants, staying out of the wind altogether.

The mountain ringlet butterfly

This butterfly lives in Scotland's mountains. It only flies for very short bursts, usually when the Sun is shining. At other times, it mainly rambles around on the ground, avoiding the high winds.

Bone breaker!

Lammergeyers are large vultures. They are skilled at finding dead animals to eat. To get at the juicy food inside a large bone, the bird carries the bone high into the air. Then it drops it onto a rock to break it up. It even eats the small pieces of shattered bone.

Mountain birds

Many mountain birds are summer visitors. They fly to warmer areas in the winter. The red-billed chough spends a lot of time on the ground searching for seeds and insects. Larger birds of **prey**, such as the peregrine falcon, eat other birds and small **mammals**. They have thick, fluffy feathers to keep out the cold.

A Web of Life

All living things in a **habitat** are connected to each other. This is because all living things need **energy** to survive. Plants get their energy from the Sun's light. They use this to make food for themselves. Some animals eat plants to get their energy. Some animals eat other animals, and some eat a mix of plants and animals. The energy in a **food chain** passes from plant to animal to animal, and so on. A food web is made of lots of connecting food chains.

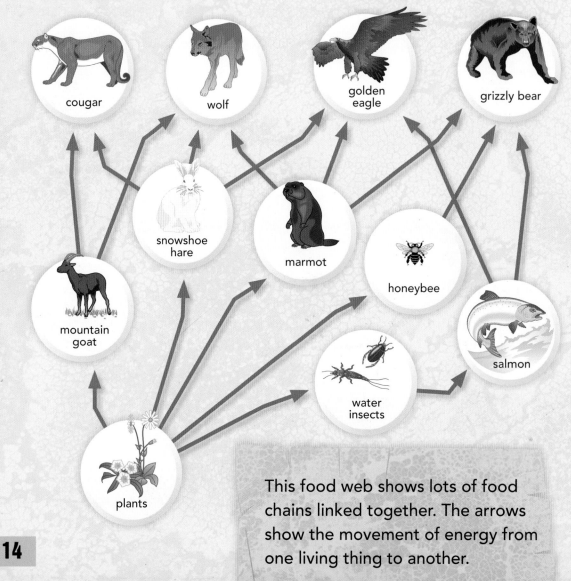

cougar

wolf

golden eagle

grizzly bear

snowshoe hare

marmot

honeybee

mountain goat

water insects

salmon

plants

This food web shows lots of food chains linked together. The arrows show the movement of energy from one living thing to another.

This marmot gets its energy from the plants it eats. The plants get their energy from the Sun's light.

Needing each other

In a mountain habitat, if one type of plant or animal becomes **extinct**, then there may be problems for other living things. For example, if the mountain cranberry plant died out, there would be less food for the bears, wolves, and snowshoe hares of the Rocky Mountains in North America.

Minibeasts have a very important role in mountain habitats. They are a source of food for birds and small **mammals**, and they help to **pollinate** flowers. They also eat dead plants and animals.

Predators and Prey

In many mountainous areas, there is not much food for the animals that live there. This is because the thin soil cannot support much plant life. This means that there are fewer herbivores (animals that eat plants). The animals that eat meat, known as carnivores, then have fewer animals to hunt.

Animals that hunt other animals are called **predators**. They have to have special skills to catch their **prey**.

Hiding to keep safe

Many prey animals use **camouflage** to hide from predators. The ptarmigan is a bird that lives in Scotland's mountains. In winter, its feathers turn white, so it can blend in with the snowy landscape. In spring, when the snow melts, the feathers turn speckled gray-brown again.

Kangaroo poo!

The female mountain katydid, a kind of grasshopper, has a clever kind of camouflage. It lies still on the ground, looking just like kangaroo droppings!

Top predators

Mountain lions are excellent hunters. They lie very still, then approach their prey quietly. Suddenly, they leap up and pounce, taking down animals as large as deer and elk.

Homes in High Places

Across the world, many people live in the mountains. Most settlements are in **valleys**, where people have some protection from the harsh weather. Valleys usually have rivers, so there is a water supply nearby. Valleys are also easier to farm and keep animals in.

Mountain people

The thin air in mountainous areas means there is less **oxygen**. Humans used to living at lower levels often feel out of breath and dizzy in the mountains. Some mountain people have **adapted** to living in this thin air.

This is a village high in the Atlas Mountains in North Africa.

Many mountain people make a living by farming. Crops such as coffee grow well in mountain areas. Farm animals such as yaks, goats, and llamas can cope with the harsh mountain environments. Today, many people work as guides and porters for the tourists who come to see the mountains.

For crops, mountain people often create stepped fields, called terraces, up mountainsides. Rice is growing in these terraces.

Threats to Mountain Habitats

Almost every mountain **range** across the world is being affected by human activity. Acid rain is a big threat to mountain forests. Acid rain is created when chemicals mix with rainwater. The chemicals come from car exhausts, factories, and power stations. When this rain falls on trees and plants, it can poison them.

These trees have been damaged by acid rain. If large areas of forest are destroyed, the whole habitat is affected.

Skiing is fun! However, it can damage the plant life under the snow. When the snow melts, fewer plants grow, so fewer insects and birds can live there.

Washing away

Some mountain **habitats** are suffering from **erosion**. This means that the soil is being washed away. This happens when trees are cut down, and when farm animals eat too many mountain plants.

Only a fly?

The meltwater stonefly likes to live in cold mountain water. Scientists in Glacier National Park in Montana have noticed that its numbers are falling. They think this is due to **global warming**. The loss of the meltwater stonefly may signal the loss of other animals.

A Big Impact

There are valuable **resources** such as coal, copper, zinc, and iron ore to be found in many mountain areas. In some areas, the mountain rock itself, such as granite and marble, can be used for building. To get these materials, the mountains must be **mined**. Some mines can destroy huge areas of **habitat**. The roads and buildings needed for the mining activities also destroy habitat.

This copper mine in Utah is one of the largest in the world.

Disappearing mountains

Mountaintop removal is a way of mining coal from mountains. However, the coal is deep below the mountain surface. To get at the coal, the top of the mountain is removed and used to fill in the mountain valleys. Many people think this should be stopped, as mountain peaks and valleys are lost forever.

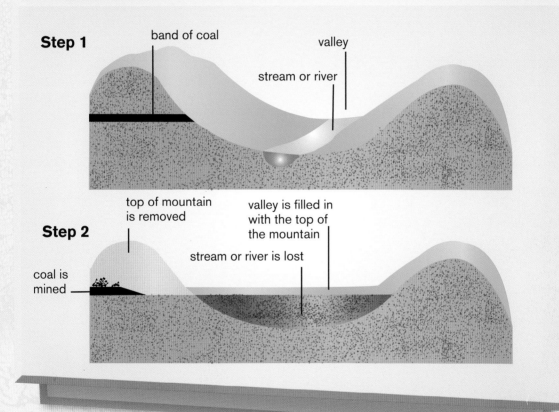

Step 1 band of coal — valley — stream or river

Step 2 top of mountain is removed — valley is filled in with the top of the mountain — stream or river is lost — coal is mined

Reservoirs

Some mountain **valleys** have been lost to reservoirs. Reservoirs are created when huge **dams** are built across rivers. This stops the flow, and the water fills up behind the dam, creating huge lakes. The water can then be used for creating electricity and for drinking. However, the valley habitat is lost.

The Struggle to Survive

When mountain **habitats** are destroyed or lost, the animals living there must move to new areas. If they move to areas where other animals already live, there may be problems with competition. Animals may fight to defend their own area, or over the food in their area. Animals that move to habitats higher up the mountain will have to cope with the harsher weather and poorer plant life.

Golden snub-nosed monkeys live in mountainous forests in China. They are becoming rare because the forests they live in are being cut down.

High fashion

People living in the Andes are finding new ways to make money. The wool from vicunas is used to make incredibly soft and warm luxury clothing. The vicuna farmers receive some of the money from selling the wool.

People who live in the mountains are making a living out of tourism. These porters are carrying equipment and supplies for mountaineers.

Back to nature

Some areas that have been cleared for an activity such as **mining** are left to go back to the wild once the mining is finished. When this happens, plants can grow again on the land. Their seeds are blown there by the wind, or carried and dropped by animals. However, this can take many years to happen.

Nature Fights Back

All over the world, nature **reserves** have been created. These reserves protect plants and animals and the **habitat** they live in.

Found!

A small tree in Mauritius was thought to be **extinct**, as it was last seen in the wild in 1863. However, in 2001, scientists discovered it growing on the island again. They have since found more trees and are now working hard to make sure the tree does not actually become extinct!

The Ladakh urial is making a comeback in Pakistan. This is because there are strict laws on hunting.

Snow leopard

The Snow Leopard Trust was set up over 30 years ago. Snow leopards in Asia were in danger from **poaching** and habitat loss. They were also being killed by farmers who feared the leopards would eat their animals. The Snow Leopard Trust works with local people to create reserves for the snow leopards.

Caledonian forest

A large mountainous area in Scotland is being replanted with ancient, **native** trees. Scots pine, alder, birch, hazel, holly, and mountain ash are being planted. This will create the perfect habitat for animals such as golden eagles, pine martens, and wildcats.

The Future for Mountain Habitats

Mountains are beautiful places. The plants and animals that live in mountain **habitats** have a special relationship with the mountain environment. A wide range of plants and animals live there. Humans also live in the mountains, but today human activity is harming mountain habitats.

How can you help?

You can do lots of things to help mountain habitats survive:

- Find out more about them—read books and research web sites.

- Join a conservation group that protects mountain species.

- Adopt an animal that lives in the mountains.

- If you visit mountains, respect the environment and do not drop litter.

- Be **energy** wise to help reduce **global warming**.

- Tell your friends and family so they can help, too.

Creating mountain paths can prevent large areas from being trampled and can direct walkers away from areas under threat.

Protecting mountains

Some of the world's last, great wild areas are in the mountains. We know that human activities may damage these, so we must work to make sure that they are protected for years to come.

Glossary

adapt change in order to survive in a particular place

camouflage color or pattern used by an animal or insect to blend into the background

continent one of Earth's seven large areas of land

dam barrier made to hold back water in a river. The dam causes the water level to rise.

energy power needed to grow, move, and live

equator imaginary line around the widest part of Earth, where the weather is always warm

erosion wearing away of Earth's surface

extinct no longer existing

food chain series of living things that provide food for each other

global warming increase in Earth's temperature, caused by chemicals in the air that trap the Sun's heat

habitat place where a plant or animal lives

mammal warm-blooded animal that usually has fur or hair and drinks milk from its mother when it is young

mining digging deep into the ground to search for substances such as coal, gemstones, and oil

native belonging to a particular country

nutrient chemical in food that helps things to grow

oxygen gas that is found in air. All living things need oxygen to survive.

poaching catching birds or animals on land belonging to someone else

pollinate carry pollen from plant to plant

predator animal that hunts and eats other animals

prey animal that is hunted and eaten by another animal

range area of connected mountains

reserve area of land set aside for the protection of plants and animals

resource something of value that can be used

valley area of low land between mountains

Find Out More

Books

Green, Jen. *Mountains Around the World* (Geography Now!). New York: PowerKids Press, 2009.

Latham, Donna. *Mountains* (Endangered Biomes). White River Junction, Vt.: Nomad Press, 2011.

Newland, Sonya. *Mountain Animals* (Saving Wildlife). Mankato, Minn.: Smart Apple Media, 2012.

Pyers, Greg. *Biodiversity of Alpine Zones.* New York: Benchmark Books, 2011.

Internet Sites

Facthound offers a safe, fun way to find Internet sites related to this book. All of the sites on Facthound have been researched by our staff.

Here's all you do:

Visit *www.facthound.com*

Type in this code: 9781410945976

Index